# CRABTREE CONTACT

# ZOMBIES ON THE LOOSE

Anne Rooney

 Crabtree Publishing Company

www.crabtreebooks.com

**Crabtree Publishing Company**
PMB 16A,
350 Fifth Avenue,
Suite 3308
New York, NY 10118

616 Welland Avenue,
St. Catharines, Ontario
L2M 5V6

Content development by
Shakespeare Squared

www.ShakespeareSquared.com

Published by Crabtree
Publishing Company © 2008

First published in Great Britain
in 2008 by ticktock Media Ltd,
2 Orchard Business Centre,
North Farm Road,
Tunbridge Wells, Kent, TN2 3XF

ticktock project editor:
  Ruth Owen
ticktock project designer:
  Sara Greasley
ticktock picture researcher:
  Lizzie Knowles

With thanks to: Series Editors Honor Head and Jean Coppendale

Picture credits (t=top; b=bottom; c=centre; l=left; r=right):
Dan Callister/ Rex Features: 31r. Nigel Catlin/ FLPA: 27. Corbis:
11 (man). John Daniels/ Alamy: 5r. David Fernandez/ epa/
Corbis: 10. Getty Images: 15. iStock: 21, 22-23, 29, 31c. Mary
Evans Picture Library/ Alamy: 19. Darby Sawchuk/ Alamy: 5l.
Shutterstock: OFC, 1, 2, 4, 8, 9, 11 (flames), 12 all, 13t, 13b, 16-
17, 22 inset, 31l. SNAP/ Rex Features: 6. Norbert Wu/ Minden
Pictures/ FLPA: 24-25.

Every effort has been made to trace copyright holders, and we
apologize in advance for any omissions. We would be pleased
to insert the appropriate acknowledgments in any subsequent
edition of this publication.

**Library and Archives Canada Cataloguing in Publication**

Rooney, Anne
    Zombies on the loose / Anne Rooney.

(Crabtree contact)
Includes index.
ISBN 978-0-7787-3767-4 (bound).--ISBN 978-0-7787-3789-6
(pbk.)

    1. Zombies--Juvenile literature. I. Title. II. Series.

GR581.R66 2008        j398'.45        C2008-901207-0

**Library of Congress Cataloging-in-Publication Data**

Rooney, Anne.
  Zombies on the loose / Anne Rooney.
    p. cm. -- (Crabtree contact)
  Includes index.
  ISBN-13: 978-0-7787-3789-6 (pbk. : alk. paper)
  ISBN-10: 0-7787-3789-6 (pbk. : alk. paper)
  ISBN-13: 978-0-7787-3767-4 (reinforced lib. bdg. : alk. paper)
  ISBN-10: 0-7787-3767-5 (reinforced lib. bdg. : alk. paper)
  1. Zombies--Juvenile literature. I. Title.
  GR581.R66 2008
  398'.45--dc22

                                        2008006290

# CONTENTS

# ZOMBIES ON THE LOOSE

You watch in horror as half-rotted creatures walk towards you.

They moan.

They groan.

These horrifying creatures are zombies.

They are coming to get you!

Thank goodness you are only watching a horror movie!

# MOVIES AND LEGENDS

In modern horror movies, rotting zombies climb out of their **graves**. They hunt and kill people to eat their **flesh**.

The first zombie movie was made in 1932. It is called *White Zombie*. In this movie, a factory owner uses zombies as **slaves**.

*White Zombie*

Zombies aren't only found in movies.
There are old **legends** about zombies, too.

Hundreds of years ago, people in Europe believed in zombies. These zombies were known as **revenants**.

People believed revenants climbed out of their graves to seek revenge on their enemies.

**Why did people believe in revenants?**

They believed in revenants because hundreds of years ago, people were sometimes buried alive by accident. If someone woke up after being buried, it seemed that he or she had come back from the dead.

# A ZOMBIE LEGEND

In the year 1090, two men died in an English village. The men were buried in the village **graveyard**.

That night, at midnight, the men were seen walking over the hills. They were carrying their **coffins** on their backs.

The men had become revenants!

Coffin

A short time after the revenants appeared, people in the village started to get sick and die. The revenants were killing them.

The villagers dug up the dead bodies. They chopped off the revenants' heads and cut out their hearts.

The village was saved!

This story is an old legend from hundreds of years ago.

But is it possible that zombies exist today?

# VOODOO ZOMBIES

Many people in Haiti, in the Caribbean, believe in **voodoo**.

Voodoo is an old African religion.

Voodoo **priestess**

In the 1700s, people were taken from Africa to Haiti to work as slaves. The slaves brought their religion with them.

Voodoo sorcerers called **bokors** create zombies.

Bokors use magic to bring zombies back from the dead. The zombies do everything the bokors tell them to do.

A Bokor

# MAKING A ZOMBIE

How do bokors turn people into zombies?

1) First, the bokor feeds a living person zombie powder — without the **victim** knowing.

Zombie powder is made from **puffer fish**, toads, poisonous tree frogs, and dead human bodies.

2) The person dies and is buried.

3) The bokor digs up the body.

4) The bokor says a spell over the dead body. The person comes back to life as a zombie.

5) The bokor feeds the zombie a special paste made from the plant zombie cucumber.

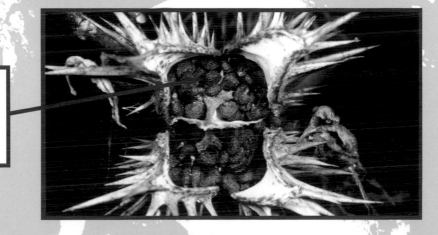

Zombie cucumber seeds

# Can a bokor really bring a dead person back to life?

Let's look at some real-life zombie stories from Haiti.

# ZOMBIE SLAVES

Bokors often make zombies to use as slaves. Sometimes bokors turn an enemy into a zombie as **revenge**.

In 1918, a bokor named Ti Joseph made a gang of nine zombies.

He made the zombies work in a **sugar cane plantation**.

Ti Joseph took all the money the zombies earned.

He treated the zombies badly and let them eat only boiled bananas.

15

# ESCAPE FROM THE SPELL

Many people believe that zombies must not eat salt or meat. If they do, it makes them aware that they are dead.

Ti Joseph's zombies ate salted nuts.

A record of what happened was written by an explorer named William Seabrook.

*"The zombies turned toward the graveyard.*

*As their cold hands touched the earth of their own graves, they fell, and lay there, rotting."*

# FELICIA – THE ZOMBIE

In 1937, something very strange happened in a small village in Haiti.

People saw an old woman walking in the street.
The woman didn't speak.
She didn't seem to know where she was.

One villager thought the woman was a member of the family. The villager thought the woman was Felicia Felix-Mentor.

Felicia became sick in 1907 when she was 29 years old. She died and her body was buried.

So how could Felicia be walking through the village 30 years later?

The villagers were frightened.

There could only be one answer.

## Felicia had come back from the dead.
## She was a zombie!

This is a photo of Felicia Felix-Mentor in 1937. Was she a real-life zombie?

# "I WAS A ZOMBIE"

A Haitian man named Clairvius Narcisse says he lived as a zombie for two years.

> **"** *I fell ill and died in hospital in 1962. I heard my sister crying when I died.*
>
> *I was buried the next day. I felt the coffin go down into my grave.*
>
> *Then my body was dug up. A bokor fed me zombie cucumber. He whipped me.*
>
> *For two years I worked in a sugar cane plantation with other zombies.*
>
> *In 1964, the bokor died. There was no more zombie cucumber. I got better!* **"**

Clairvius returned to his family in 1982 — 20 years after he died!

# DON'T BE A ZOMBIE

Some people in Haiti are afraid that they might come back from the dead as zombies.

To stop this from happening, they asked to be buried under heavy stones when they died.

Sometimes, the doors of Haitian tombs are locked with padlocks. **The locks are meant to stop bokors from removing bodies from graves.**

Padlock

# ARE ZOMBIES REAL?

Can a bokor really make a zombie? Some experts believe that science has the answer.

The Haitian puffer fish contains a deadly poison.
The poison can be made into a powder.

The powder **paralyzes** anyone who eats it.
The person's breathing slows down.
The person's heartbeat nearly stops.

## The victim seems dead!

But when the poison wears off, the person
comes back to life.

Could poison from puffer
fish explain stories of people
coming back from the dead?

The zombie cucumber is a poisonous plant.

Zombie cucumber can make a person go mad. It can make them forget everything. The person doesn't know what they're doing!

Someone who ate zombie cucumber could be controlled by a bokor.

In Haiti, many people have strong beliefs in zombies.

When this belief is mixed with strong poisons, a person might begin to believe that he or she is a zombie.

A zombie cucumber plant

# FELICIA – THE TRUTH

The zombie Felicia Felix-Mentor was examined by a doctor.

The doctor found that the strange woman was not the real Felicia.

He said the zombie-like woman had a **mental illness**. That was why she didn't speak.

Felicia had been **lame** before her death. The zombie-like woman couldn't walk very well. Felicia's family thought this was proof it was Felicia. But the woman was just weak from not eating.

# NEED-TO-KNOW WORDS

**bokor** A sorcerer, or magician, who turns people into zombies

**coffin** A box that holds a dead body

**flesh** The soft parts of a body including muscle and fat

**grave** A hole in the ground where a body is buried

**graveyard** An area where many bodies are buried

**lame** Unable to walk properly because of an injury to a foot or leg

**legend** A story that is passed down through history

**mental illness** A health condition that affects a person's thoughts, emotions, and/or behavior

**paralyzes** To make unable to move

**priestess** A woman who presides over religious ceremonies

**puffer fish** A fish that puffs up its body when it is attacked. Many parts of the puffer fish contain a very strong poison.

**revenge** To do something bad to someone because he or she did something bad to you

**slave** A person who belongs to another person and has to work for him or her

**sorcerer** Someone who has magic powers

**sugar cane plantation** A field where a type of grass is grown. Sugar is made from the stems of the grass.

**victim** The person who has suffered an injury or death as a result of an accident, or what someone else has done

**voodoo** An African religion involving magic

**zombie** A person who is thought to be dead but is able to walk around

# ZOMBIE SPOTTER'S GUIDE

### Revenant
- Lived in Europe hundreds of years ago
- Rotting skin
- Bones sticking out
- Has maggots eating its body
- Carries its coffin wherever it goes

### Voodoo zombie
- Lives in Haiti
- Not rotting
- Has normal skin
- Has staring eyes
- It doesn't speak
- Is controlled by a bokor

### Movie zombie
- Can live anywhere
- Rotting skin
- Eats human flesh
- Moves slowly but can carry on even if hurt
- Moans and groans

# ZOMBIES ONLINE

## Websites

http://science.howstuffworks.com/zombie.htm
Information about the history of zombies

http://zombies.tomwalsham.com/costume.html
How to do zombie make-up and costumes

http://zombies.monstrous.com
Information about different types of zombies

**Publisher's note to educators and parents:**
Our editors have carefully reviewed these websites to ensure that they are suitable for children. Many websites change frequently, however, and we cannot guarantee that a site's future contents will continue to meet our high standards of quality and educational value. Be advised that children should be closely supervised whenever they access the Internet.

# INDEX

Printed in the U.S.A.